TIGER

The production of this book has
been generously supported by the
Simon Gibson Charitable Trust,
The Iliffe Family Charitable Trust,
the Manifold Trust and the
Rothschild Foundation.
Many many thanks to them all.

For Gabriel

Animals in Art

TIGER

by Joanna Skipwith

Silver Jungle

DEAR READER

Is this book suitable for you? I hope so. Its purpose is very simple. Its purpose is to make you fall in love, *even more*, with the tiger, whatever age you are, and to remind you just how much we will miss it. The text was written with a nine-year-old in mind, a boy who already seems to know what predator, dissection, even carnassial mean, but has no idea about 'satin'. I hope, however, that there will be something here for all ages. If you are very young and still teething, you have probably started to enjoy the hardback corners already. If you are a little older and like looking at pictures, then perhaps you can count the tigers and see which parts of the world they have come from. There are at least 23 different artists from 12 different countries.

For readers, there may be some tricky words such as 'symmetry' and 'disconcerting' lurking in the text. There may be some in Greek, even Hindi. I do apologise. You don't have to read them. For the 'mature' reader, I hope that many of the pictures and some of the information will come as a surprise.

Tibetan artist
An illustration from *Folk-tales from Tibet* by Captain O'Connor, 1906. The artist's name is not given.

Tigers have inspired writers and artists for many centuries in many different cultures. Powerful and beautiful, seemingly proud loners, they are symbols of courage and bravery in the East. In the West, they are used to sell all sorts of things including petrol, tea and breakfast cereals. Images of them multiply and multiply in children's books, in animated films and in advertising. They have become very familiar to us, but the real animals – dangerous, wild, independent – are very unfamiliar to most people, and their numbers are decreasing every day. There are five subspecies, all endangered, some very likely to disappear without an enormous amount of money and work.

How this book was made
This book was printed in England on Revive Special Silk by Beacon Press using *pure*print environmental print technology. The paper, which combines recycled waste paper and new fibre from well-managed forests, is approved by the Forest Stewardship Council.

TIGER

The tiger conjures up different images for different people. For some it is an overgrown kitten with pale amber eyes, superior whiskers and soft boxing paws, something you might be tempted to stroke if only you were allowed to. For others it is terrifying, an orange shredding machine with the sharpest claws of all carnivores. Two famous tigers adopted by Disney and included in this book show opposite aspects of the fictional tiger. The happy-go-lucky Tigger bounces his way into our hearts, whilst the cunning Shere Kahn remains aloof and intent on killing Mowgli.

For the Ancient Romans, tigers represented untamed nature, yet another thing that had to be conquered and put in its place. Large numbers of tigers were captured, together with other wild animals, and shipped back to Rome. They were expected to perform in the amphitheatres, in circuses and staggeringly brutal shows that celebrated military victories and religious festivals. Animals and gladiators were encouraged to tear each other apart, and *thousands* of animals were killed at a time. Oh those revolting Ancient Romans. Thank heavens they are now extinct.

Tiger and its tamer
Roman mosaic, 1st century AD
Museo Nazionale delle Terme, Rome

Romans used mosaics to decorate the floors, walls and ceilings of their villas and temples. The small glazed squares were made from tiles and fragments of broken pottery. Some mosaics were standard designs bought from shops and chosen from pattern books, rather like wallpaper today. Others were designed specially for the owners and were usually the most important decorative feature of a villa.

TERRITORY

The tiger's habitat used to range from eastern Turkey through to the north-west regions of China, up into the snow-covered cedar forests of Siberia and south through China to the tropical islands of Sumatra, Java and Bali. They used to pad silently after wild boar along the Persian shores of the Caspian Sea, they crept through the jungles of bamboo and silk-cotton trees in Assam, some followed roe deer just below the snow line of the Himalayas and others tiptoed along the sand under the stars in Bali. But now they are restricted to pockets of southern and eastern Asia, in game reserves or areas that humans have not yet occupied. They tend to live in dense forests or areas with tall grasses – grasses that can hide them from their prey.

Shy, nocturnal animals, the adults usually live alone and establish their own territories. They tend not to overlap those of the same sex and ensure this by spraying urine on rocks and trees along the boundaries. The size of a territory depends on how much prey there is. In parts of India where there are plenty of deer, a male tiger may need as little as 10 square miles (26 km²). In the Russian Far East, where prey is scattered over a wide area and may move each season, a male tiger can cover a range of 400 square miles (1036 km²).

Kano Sanraku
Japanese, 1559–1635
Dragon of the Storm, Tiger with Bamboo
Ink and colours on paper
Detail from one of a pair of screens
Myoshin-ji Temple, Kyoto, Japan

Tigers have never lived in Japan. Their images were copied from Chinese artists, who often depicted them as one of four animals that guarded the compass points – North, South, East and West. The tiger represented the West, the dragon the East. They often appear in Japanese temples, on folding screens or *fusuma* (paper-covered sliding doors). Kano Sanraku was responsible for some of the finest screens of the early Edo period, often painted on gold leaf. As in early Ming paintings from China, Sanraku painted the male tiger with stripes and the female with spots. Although this is incorrect, they make a very attractive couple.

FIVE TIGERS

The tiger is the largest of the big cats, but as the five subspecies vary in size and weight, the average tiger is about the same size as a lion. Females of each subspecies are usually smaller than the males.

The **Amur** (also known as the Siberian tiger) is the largest and heaviest. It lives mainly in the forests of the Russian Far East. It is the palest in colour with the thickest coat, to protect it from the cold in winter. There are approximately 400 left in the wild, more in captivity.

The **Indian** (also known as the Bengal tiger) is the most common. It is estimated that there are 3–5,000 living in the wild. Most live in India, some are found in Nepal, Bangladesh, Bhutan and Myanmar (Burma).

The range of the **Indochinese** tiger includes the mountainous remote forests of Cambodia, Myanmar, Laos, Vietnam and Malaysia. It is difficult to monitor them; numbers are estimated at 1–2,000.

The **South China** tiger survives only in captivity. Although it has not been seen in the wild for 10 years, it is not officially extinct. All the subspecies are thought to have descended from this tiger.

The **Sumatran** is the smallest and has the darkest coat. It lives only in Sumatra, and there may be as few as 400 left.

Eric Wilson
British, b. 1960
Detail from *Taiga Tiger*, 1998
Oil on board
Private Collection

This is not a photograph, though it is hard to believe. It is an oil painting that took eight weeks to complete, beginning with sketches and photographs of an Amur tiger. The artist then slowly created the forest of larch and silver birch trees, working from the background to the large trees in the foreground. The colour was built up slowly in thin glazes to create the appearance of a snowy landscape illuminated by sunlight, and as the painting progressed the brushes used became smaller and smaller. The setting was created from the artist's imagination, though he has visited eastern Russia and made many sketches of its remote wilderness.

SABRE-TOOTH TIGER

The fabled sabre-tooth tiger was a smilodon, a large prehistoric cat that became extinct about 10,000 years ago. Scientists now believe that it was not the ancestor of today's tiger, not a tiger at all in fact. It was slightly smaller than a lion but much heavier, with shorter legs and a bobbed tail. Its huge canine teeth were serrated and grew up to 18 cm (7 in) long.

The character of Diego in the film *Ice Age* has a heart of gold hidden behind those ferocious fangs and sly exterior. Like the best tigers and the nicest of villains, he overcomes his predatory instincts and becomes a true friend to Manfred the mammoth and Sid the sloth.

Smilodon comes from the Greek words *smile* meaning knife and *odous, odontos* meaning tooth. Perhaps it inspired this famous and anonymous limerick.

There was a young lady from Niger
Who smiled as she rode on a tiger.
They returned from the ride
With the lady inside,
And the smile on the face of the tiger.

Diego, Sid and Manny in *Ice Age*
Directed by Chris Wedge and Carlos Saldanha. Created by Blue Sky Studios
©2002 Twentieth Century Fox

Ice Age is a digital animated feature film. There are 24 'frames' for each second of the film and each one requires the input of a team of artists working in character design, set design, modelling, animation, special effects and lighting. Every aspect of Diego's appearance, every hair on his body, the glint in his eye, the curl of his lip, is created by a team of people over several months. Lights, fur, ACTION!

EARS, NOSE AND THROAT

Ears: two swivelling ones, all the better for hearing you. And all the better for listening to the footsteps of different types of prey. The white spots on the backs of the ears look to other animals like eyes and may help to deter anything planning to creep up from behind.

Eyes: two beautiful amber ones, all the better for seeing you. Tigers have the brightest eyes of all mammals. Their night vision is excellent, six times better than that of humans.

Nose: one small pink one, all the better for smelling you. A tiger relies less on smell than other hunting animals. It uses its nose to sniff the scents of other tigers, to find out where they are and how recently they have passed through an area. A 'Keep Out' message left in the urine of a male tiger will avoid unnecessary conflict. 'Come and Get Me', left by a female, will let the local males know that she is ready to mate.

Teeth: 30, all the better for eating you, my dear. The huge front fangs, or canines, stab the prey and keep a tight grip. The side carnassials are for slicing meat into chunks to swallow (cats cannot chew), and the large molars are for grinding and crushing. Quite large bones are swallowed whole. The small front incisors help to scrape the last bits from the carcass.

Gary Stinton
British, b. 1961
Detail from *Siberian Tiger*, 2004
Pastel on paper
Private Collection, Italy

Gary Stinton specialises in painting big cats and fox-hounds. He works in pastels as they capture the pelt of the animals in a realistic way. This is a detail from a life-size drawing, and its owner finds it a rather disturbing companion. Note that the ears are pointing back. If the tiger feels threatened or hostile it can rotate its ears back, bringing the white spots forward. If you look at the ears in the other pictures, you will get a sense of the tigers' different moods.

PAWS AND CLAWS

Skin: one loose stripy one, like a velvety jumpsuit covering its powerful muscles. It will stretch easily when the tiger leaps and runs, and can be pulled in fights without tearing.

Legs: four, short for the size of the body but very powerful. The front legs and shoulders (used to pull down prey) are heavily muscled. The back legs, which provide the spring before an attack, are slightly longer. A tiger can leap 4.5 metres (15 ft) and run fast, but it cannot run far without getting tired.

Toes: eighteen. 18? $18 \div 4 = 4\frac{1}{2}$? Yes, but the tiger has five toes on its front paws (one much shorter, like a thumb) and only four on its back paws. Its footprint is called a 'pug mark'.

Claws: eighteen, the sharpest claws of all carnivores. They slip back into sheaths when they are not needed. They cannot be flicked out at will (as Shere Khan does most impressively in Disney's *The Jungle Book*). This happens automatically as the tiger stretches out to spring at its victim or reaches up to sharpen them on a tree trunk.

Tail: one long swishing one. It can measure as much as 120 cm (4 ft) long, about half the length of the tiger's body. It helps to balance the tiger as it leaps and turns.

Sir Edwin Landseer
British, 1802–73
Study of a Tiger, c. 1820
Pencil and watercolour on paper
British Museum, London

Edwin Landseer was famous for his paintings of animals. He was a 'child prodigy' and first exhibited at the Royal Academy when he was 12. He particularly enjoyed drawing tigers and lions and is known to have dissected them in order to understand the relationship of muscles and sinews. Queen Victoria's favourite painter, he designed the group of lions at the foot of Nelson's column in Trafalgar Square, London.

WHY DO TIGERS HAVE STRIPES?

Why *do* tigers have stripes? Stripes help to break up the outline of the tiger's body and provide ideal camouflage in long grass and in the dappled shade of the forest. Animals see fewer colours than we do, especially nocturnal animals. At dusk and dawn, when tigers are most active, light levels will be poor. The green jungle will become a mass of flickering shadows, and a grey stripy tiger crouching silently behind grey stripy grass will be very difficult for another animal to see.

The stripes vary in colour, size and in the way they split and divide. No two tigers have the same pattern; this is particularly noticeable in the black and white markings on the forehead. Underneath the furry stripes, the skin is striped as well. If you shave a tiger (DO NOT, I repeat NOT attempt this at home, not even under adult supervision), the stripes will still be there on the surface of the skin.

The different subspecies have adapted to different climates. In the Russian Far East, the Amur tiger needs long fur to provide warmth in very cold winters, though it also has a summer coat. The tigers living in India, however, need only short fur. Sometimes orange, sometimes golden brown, with brown or black stripes, the coat of a healthy tiger ripples like satin.

Henri Rousseau
French, 1844–1910
Tiger in a Tropical Storm, 1891
Oil on canvas
National Gallery, London

Rousseau was a self-taught artist, who retired early from his job as inspector at a toll-station outside Paris. Rousseau never went to the jungles of southern India. He created his paintings from his imagination, drawing animals in the Paris zoo, the *Jardin des Plantes*, and borrowing ideas from book illustrations and displays at the natural history museum.

Henri Rousseau

LOVE OF WATER

Tigers love water. In the tropical jungles they need to cool down and will spend many an hour lying in shallow streams and pools during the hot weather. They often enter the water backwards as they like to keep their eyes and whiskers dry. They have fun and go swimming, and have been known to cross a distance of 5 miles (8 km). In the deltas of the Ganges and in the Sunderbans mangroves they swim from island to island, and some believe that they first swam to Sumatra from the Malay Peninsula.

Thirsty carnivores must never be too far from fresh drinking water, and tigers will travel great distances to find it during the drought periods. Whether stream, reed bed or water hole, the water's edge is a good place to lie in wait for an evening meal as many other animals, including deer, will drop by for a drink. Unfortunately, as water is a lure for both the tiger and its prey, it is an obvious place for poachers to set their traps.

Tim Warnes and Jane Chapman
British
Detail from *My Reflection*
©Tim Warnes/Jane Chapman, 1996

Husband and wife, Tim Warnes and Jane Chapman met at art school and have worked alongside each other since 1994, illustrating children's books for several publishers. They usually work separately, but both had a hand in creating this picture for a greetings card, which was sold in aid of Greenpeace. Tim is best known for illustrating the *Little Tiger* series for Little Tiger Press. Jane has worked for many publishers, sometimes using the pseudonym Jack Tickle.

POUNCE!

Unlike lions, which hunt as a team, the tiger hunts alone. It does not have the speed of a cheetah so it must get as close as it can to its prey. It creeps up as quietly as possible, moving very slowly, avoiding the crackle of dead leaves or the snap of a twig under its paws. It must take its prey by surprise for once it has pounced there is sure to be a commotion. The herd will dart away on thundering hooves, beady-eyed monkeys will scramble and shriek through the trees, alerting the rest of the forest. If the prey gets away, the tiger will have to wait a very long time until it gets another opportunity. There are no snacks between meals for the wild tiger – no tinned cat food left by the back door. It must kill every time it wants to eat.

Tigers attack from behind. They bring their prey down with their strong forelegs and usually sink their teeth into the animal's neck to deliver the final blow. They will kill animals as big as themselves, elephant calves even a large crocodile, but they cannot afford to take too many risks. An injured tiger will not be able to hunt for food and could starve before it recovers.

Eugène Delacroix
French, 1798–1863
Tiger Attacking a Wild Horse, c. 1826–29
Watercolour
Musée du Louvre, Paris

Delacroix is regarded as one of France's greatest painters and was praised by the poet Baudelaire as a genius of modern art. His paintings have tremendous energy and passion, many on a huge scale, tackling French history, massacre and revolution. He loved painting tigers and lions, and visited them frequently at the Paris zoo. He would then unleash them in his paintings. One art critic, who knew Delacroix well, thought that he looked like a cat. He had 'tawny feline eyes with thick, arched brows, and a face of wild and disconcerting beauty, yet he could be as soft as velvet, and could be stroked and caressed like one of those tigers'.

BREAKFAST, AT LAST

Once the tiger has caught breakfast, it will drag the carcass to a safe place to enjoy it in peace. A mother will share the kill with her cubs, but otherwise tigers prefer to eat alone. They are not fussy eaters and will eat the meat, skin AND bones. They do not rush their food and will spend a long time preparing the carcass. Sometimes they bite off the tail and put it to one side. Then they usually begin with rump and thigh, ending with the innards – intestines, liver and heart. After a meal, they lick away all the blood from their fur with their rough tongues. They would soon be surrounded by flies if they did not clean themselves thoroughly.

A tiger eats up to 35 kg (77 lb) of meat at a time, alternating gorges with lean periods between kills. It needs an average of 7 kg (15 lb) of meat a day, which means that it must kill a medium-sized animal about once a week.

Tigers eat what is available in their area, but different species of deer and wild pig form the main part of their diet. Monkeys are added to the menu in Indonesia, even the odd tapir or porcupine. Tigers that live in the mangrove swamps also catch frogs, fish and crabs in the shallow water.

Gennadi Pavlishin
Russian, b. 1938
Illustration for *Golden Rigma*
by Vsevolod Sysoev
Published by Riotip, Khabarovsk, 1998

Gennadi Pavlishin grew up in far eastern Russia, land of the Amur tiger. He has illustrated several books about Russian wildlife and local customs, and his love of the countryside is clear in every detail. How many tigers are there in this painting? Are you sure? If you look closely you will find Rigma, an orphaned cub, waiting for a small but very unlikely share of another family's kill.

'That Autumn, brown bears were short of food and didn't go to their lairs to hibernate. One always followed the tiger family to feed on what was left from their meals ... He had claws as long as daggers, and they clicked like castanets whenever he walked along a well-trodden boar path or a frozen river.'

HOW TO CATCH A TIGER

Hunting tigers has been popular since primitive man first killed them for their skins, and different methods have evolved over the centuries. An unusual one for capturing a cub is often shown in medieval bestiaries. The hunter attempting to steal a cub knows that his horse may not outrun an enraged mother. He drops a large glass ball to distract her. Confused by her own shrunken image in the curved glass, the tigress mistakes her reflection for the cub and attempts to lick it protectively. This clever but rotten trick also appears in a Roman mosaic in Sicily, though it is not known whether such a tactic was used or was effective.

In reality, most tigresses show great intelligence and bravery when protecting their cubs. On average there are two or three in a litter, though there can be as many as six. They are very vulnerable when their mother is away, but she must leave them to hunt. She is careful not to lead predators to them, choosing stony rather than soft ground to avoid leaving footprints. She varies her hunting time and moves the cubs if necessary, carrying them by their necks in her mouth.

A tigress cannot afford a long pregnancy. It will slow her down, and she needs her speed and power to hunt. She usually carries her cubs for about 15 weeks, a short gestation for such a large mammal.

Tiger and cub
Detail from a page in the Worksop Bestiary, an English manuscript dating back to the 12th century
The Pierpoint Morgan Library, New York
MS M.81 f. 35

Bestiaries were an early form of natural history, which documented animals, both real and imagined ones, giving information about their habits and telling stories that might help people to understand their own behaviour and lead better lives. In the Middle Ages, when this illustration was made, the text was written in Latin with a sharpened quill or reed pen. The pictures were sometimes 'illuminated' with gold or silver. This bestiary is one of the earliest, and this page with the tiger was once owned by the British artist and poet William Morris, famous for his richly patterned wallpaper designs.

mortuos sepelire mortuos. tu au uade. seqre me.

Tigris uocata ppt uolucre fugã. ita ĥ no
minant pse. greci. œ medi saguttã. ht enĩ
bestia uariis distincta maclis. uirtut'z uelo

BEFORE IT CATCHES YOU

At the time of this painting, hunting tigers was an exclusive sport, reserved for royal families and their guests. Indian princes were expected to demonstrate their courage and prove themselves fit leaders by 'bagging' a tiger, trapping it with nets and then killing it, with spears or arrows. Visiting royalty and noblemen would be taken along on elephants or horseback. No doubt there were times when things did not go as planned.

In the late 19th century, the spears and arrows were replaced with guns, and shooting tigers became a favourite pastime of the British army officers living in India. Elaborate hunting expeditions were organised, and beaters would clatter through the forests banging pots and pans, shooing tigers from their hiding places.

The Second World War spread troops and guns far and wide across Asia. The guns remained and hunting big game increased dramatically. As tigers became more and more scarce, there was a sense of urgency, not to conserve them, but for hunters from all over the world to come and collect their trophies. Elephants and beaters were replaced with jeeps and spotlights so that tigers could be shot at night. Hunting tigers was eventually banned in India in 1971.

Peter Paul Rubens
Flemish, 1577–1640
The Tiger Hunt, c. 1616
Oil on canvas
Musée des Beaux-Arts, Rennes, France

Rubens was one of the busiest and most energetic artists in the history of art. Trained in Antwerp, he became court painter to the Duke of Mantua in Italy and later to the Spanish governors of the Netherlands. He employed many talented assistants to complete the commissions that poured in, overseeing production and usually adding the finishing touches. His patrons often wanted hunting scenes: a little action, a touch of horror and a riot of exotic beasts. This painting was commissioned by Maximilian I, Duke of Bavaria. The strange mixture of animals may have been sketched from life in a nobleman's menagerie, but they would not have been found together in the wild.

THE TYGER

Tyger Tyger, burning bright,
In the forests of the night:
What immortal hand or eye,
Could frame thy fearful symmetry?

In what distant deeps or skies,
Burnt the fire of thine eyes?
On what wings dare he aspire?
What the hand, dare seize the fire?

And what shoulder, & what art,
Could twist the sinews of thy heart?
And when thy heart began to beat,
What dread hand? & what dread feet?

What the hammer? what the chain,
In what furnace was thy brain?
What the anvil? what dread grasp,
Dare its deadly terrors clasp?

When the stars threw down their spears
And water'd heaven with their tears:
Did he smile his work to see?
Did he who made the Lamb make thee?

Tyger Tyger, burning bright,
In the forests of the night:
What immortal hand or eye,
Dare frame thy fearful symmetry?

Khwan Plykeaw-Barton
Thai, b. 1973
Bengal Tiger in the Jungle, 1998
Oil on canvas

William Blake's famous poem was
written as part of a collection of poems,
Songs of Experience, published in 1794.
The devilish 'manufacture' of the tiger is
in direct contrast to his poem 'The Lamb'
in *Songs of Innocence*. The tiger that Blake
drew himself to illustrate his poem does
not burn bright, nor does it have fearful
symmetry. It looks rather dozy and
appears to be posing beside a deciduous
tree in broad daylight. So, with many
apologies to a very talented and famous
artist, I have illustrated his poem instead
with a contemporary painting by Khwan
Plykeaw-Barton who has studied tigers
in Thailand.

Poem by **William Blake**
British poet and artist 1757–1827

FATAL COMBAT

Animals have been admired in captivity for many centuries, since the time of the Ancient Egyptians and Queen Hatshepsut, and of the early Chinese emperors. By the 13th century, exotic wild animals were often given as gifts from one ruler to another, and these gifts had to be housed. A royal menagerie (as the early private zoos were called) was established at the Tower of London by Henry III. He had been given three leopards in 1235. Henry sometimes staged fights between tigers and lions, for private amusement, and this tradition continued into Elizabethan times. Later, the Tower and its animals were opened to the public on a regular basis, and it was here that William Blake first saw a tiger.

In an incident recorded in the newspapers in 1830, a cleaner made the mistake of opening the door that connected the lion's cage to that of the tiger and tigress. The lion promptly slunk through, sprang at the tiger and an almighty battle began. Fur flew and the three animals made such a tremendous noise that all the other caged animals – including panthers, bears and hyenas – roared and howled in terror. The tigers won but had to be restrained with red-hot iron pokers. (YIKES!) The lion was called George. He was very badly mauled ... but before you start feeling too sorry for him, just remember who started it.

Extraordinary and Fatal Combat, 1830
Lithograph published by S. Maunder
Guildhall Library, City of London

A new printing technique called lithography was invented in 1798 and enabled artists to become more involved in the production of their prints. First the artist would draw an image in oil on a smooth piece of limestone, then acid was used to burn the oil into the stone. As oil and water do not mix, some areas of the stone were then treated with water to repel the oil-based inks and other areas were treated to retain the ink. A separate stone was used for each colour, and the print was pressed on to each slab, slowly building up the picture each time. The furry battle at the Tower of London must have been a talking point, and perhaps several people wanted an image of it.

LOVED AND FEARED

The tiger used to be very important in different Asian cultures. Wherever it roamed, whether China, Korea, Vietnam or India, stories and myths developed, stories of white tigers, blue tigers, magical tigers, tigers that could transport people from this world to an after-life, people that could turn into tigers if they ate the right kind of rice.

Loved and feared in India and Bangladesh for centuries by Hindus and Muslims, tigers are still regarded as 'brother', protector and guardian of the forests. For those that lived alongside them, the tigers' dominance of the jungles and their connection with nature was treated with great respect. It was recognised that they were somehow inseparable from their habitat. Though known to be powerful aggressive animals, they were first and foremost symbols of positive change: new life, balance, peace and fertility.

The Hindu goddess Durga is frequently shown riding a tiger or a lion. Not only strong, these animals were chosen to carry her because they could guide and protect her in her fight against evil. Durga's name means 'Beyond Reach', and it is possible that she was paired with a tiger because it, too, was considered beyond man's reach, before the invention of the gun.

Lady with Attendants, c. 1800
Detail of a scroll painting
West Bengal, gouache on paper
©V&A Images/Victoria and Albert Museum

In this detail of a scroll painting the two stylised tigers guard a pregnant woman and bring her luck. In a lower section of the scroll, not shown here, the mother has given birth and is nursing her tiny newborn baby. At the time of this painting, the Bengali people believed that tigers could help women to bear children. The two serpents (cobras) are also symbols of fertility. They were believed to be guardians of the earth's greatest secret, the secret of Creation.

MAN-EATER

Very few tigers become man-eaters, but those that do are terrifying neighbours to live alongside. Attacks on humans usually arise when tigers are forced to live too close to us, when prey is scarce and tigers are starving. Then, for old and injured tigers unable to hunt, or young inexperienced ones, we become fair game. Some do eat people, however, without much of an excuse.

The tigers in the Sunderbans are the most notorious killers. The Sunderbans is a huge area of forest at the mouth of the Ganges, stretching across the borders of India and Bangladesh. It floods with sea water and much of it is uninhabited, but people venture in to fish and to collect wood and honey. Unfortunately the tigers here have developed a taste for them. Braver woodcutters and fisherman, prepared to take the risk, wear masks on the backs of their heads to fool the tigers into believing that they are being watched. As tigers always attack from behind, this was effective for a while, but the cunning ones have already realised the trick.

Some believe that a salty diet is to blame. Fresh water is scarce in this area, and the tigers have adapted to drinking salt water, which may make them unnaturally aggressive. Yes, that must be it. It must be the salt, surely?

Salvador Dalí
Spanish, 1904–1989
Dream caused by the flight of a bee around a pomegranate one second before waking, 1944. Oil on canvas, Thyssen-Bornemisza Collection, Madrid, Spain

Dalí described his works as 'hand-painted dream photographs'. He was a Surrealist, and the Surrealist poets and artists encouraged each other to pay attention to their dreams and to find a deeper reality by exploring their imaginations. Independent as a tiger, Dalí was expelled from art school after announcing that none of his tutors were good enough to examine him. He was even expelled from the Surrealist group. His response, naturally, was to say: 'The only difference between me and the Surrealists is that I am a Surrealist.' Proud, too. This painting could mean all sorts of things. Natural forms evolve from one another: the pomegranate, the fish and the tiger. Then comes the man-made rifle with its bayonet, which is about to jab the sleeping woman. She dreams peacefully as the ice sheet cracks beneath her and floods the landscape?

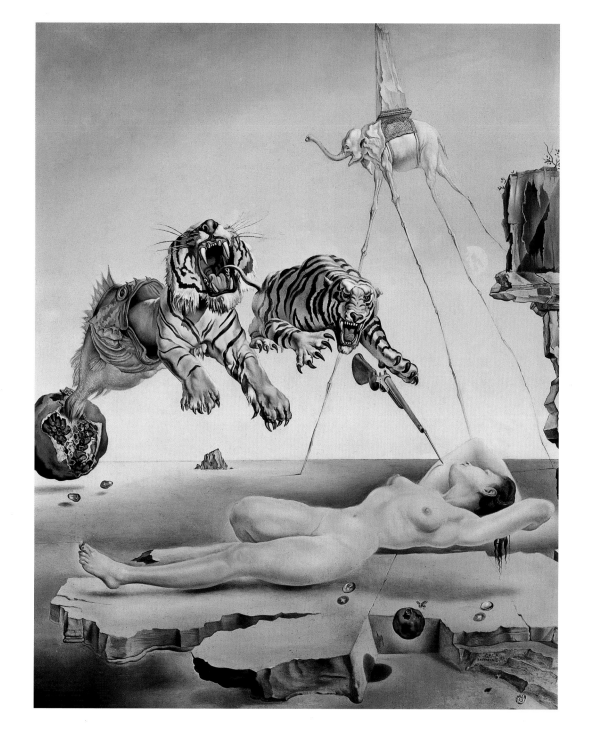

SHERE KHAN

Of all the man-eating tigers, Shere Khan, the lame tiger in *The Jungle Book*, is perhaps the best known. Written by Rudyard Kipling, who was born in India, and published in 1894, *The Jungle Book* includes stories about Mowgli, the man cub who is reared by wolves, guided by Bagheera the panther and Baloo the bear, and stalked by the menacing Shere Khan.

The Disney adaptation is based on two stories, *Mowgli's Brothers* and *Kaa's Hunting*, in which Mowgli manages to keep the tiger at bay, using fire to scare him away. In the later story *Tiger! Tiger!*, whose title derives from Blake's poem, Mowgli traps Shere Khan in a ravine with the help of the wolves, Akela and Grey Brother. Together they create a buffalo stampede, which tramples Shere Khan to death. Another familiar film sequence perhaps, and familiar names if you are a cub or scout?

Sher is the Indian (Hindi) name for tiger, and Sher Khan was a famous Afghan ruler who took control of the Mughal Empire from 1540 to 1545. However, it was probably a later Afghan ruler, and a contemporary of Kipling's, who inspired the choice of name: Sher Khan Nasher (most appropriate for a tiger).

Shere Khan and Kaa, likeable rogues
From *The Jungle Book*, 1967
©Disney Enterprises, Inc.

William Blake, Rudyard Kipling, Walt Disney – three important creative talents in the life of the tiger. *The Jungle Book* was the last animated film that Walt Disney supervised, and he died prior to its release. He discouraged his animators from reading Kipling's story as he wanted them to create something modern. Shere Khan was drawn by Milt Kahl (1909–87), considered by many to be Disney's best draughtsman and one of the greatest animators. His imagination and skill, together with the powerful haughty voice of English actor George Sanders, make Shere Khan a most memorable baddy. Kaa, the snake, was one of Disney's favourite characters. He almost steals the show.

THE THREAT OF EXTINCTION

As with many endangered animals, the threat to tigers comes from man, from our management and modernisation of the natural world. We have cleared large areas of land for agriculture and development, shot tigers like vermin and pushed them to the margins of their habitat. The very things we most admire about them, their distinctive skins, their ferocity and their independence, have caused many to want to control them, own them, even eat them, in the hope of gaining something of their power and mystery. All parts of the tiger's body are used in traditional Chinese medicine, and the demand for these medicines is as high as ever. Bones are thought to cure rheumatism, whiskers are thought to help toothache, the brain is meant to cure laziness and pimples.

Fifty years ago there were eight subspecies. Today there are five, *just*. There are international campaigns to protect them, anti-poaching task forces, laws that ban the export of their body parts, and attempts to replace tiger medicines with alternative remedies. In spite of this, Indian tigers are still poached from the very parks and reserves set up to protect them. In China, almost extinct in the wild, they are 'farmed' in the hope that the bone trade will be legalised again.

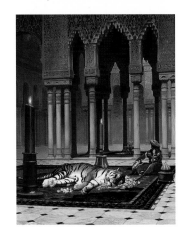

Jean-Léon Gérôme
French, 1824–1904
The Grief of the Pasha, 1882
Oil on canvas
Joslyn Art Museum, Omaha, Nebraska, USA. Gift of Francis T. B. Martin (1990.1)

The French artist Gérôme created many exotic scenes from his imagination, but the architecture and objects included are painted in such detail and with such accuracy that they make a convincing picture. This painting of a Turkish pasha with his Nubian tiger uses the Alhambra Palace in Spain as the setting. It was commissioned to illustrate a poem by Victor Hugo, *The Grief of the Pasha*. In it Hugo wonders why this wealthy commander of the Turkish army is so sad. He has not witnessed the destruction of cities and the slaughter of his people. No, the pasha weeps because his pet tiger has died. Tigers became one of Gérôme's favourite subjects.

TIGGER

In *The House at Pooh Corner* Tigger is the bouncing, boastful outsider. The other animals have no idea where he has come from or what he eats for breakfast (nor does Tigger), but despite Eeyore and Rabbit's reservations he is undoubtedly a cheerful addition to the forest. Although Tigger has very different habits from tigers in the wild – he likes malt extract – he does share some of their characteristics. He can swim and he can climb trees, upwards. As Roo points out, Tiggers can't climb downwards because their tails get in the way. This makes perfect sense to me, but tigers do in fact climb down backwards, using their curved claws to keep a tight hold. What tigers and tiggers seem to do best is pouncing, or bouncing.

Pooh first meets Tigger in the middle of the night. Woken by his yowlings, Pooh politely invites him in to sleep on the floor. The following morning he finds his new friend looking at a reflection of himself in the mirror. 'Hallo!' said Tigger. 'I've found somebody just like me. I thought I was the only one of them.'

What if? What if there was only one tiger left? It is hard to imagine, for as we all know ... the wonderful thing about tigers is tigers are wonderful things.

Ernest H. Shepard
British, 1879–1976
*'We can't get down, we can't get down!'
cried Roo*. Colour sketch for *The World of Pooh* by A. A. Milne, first published by E.P. Hutton, New York, 1957

A. A. Milne wrote *Winnie the Pooh* and *The House at Pooh Corner* for his son Christopher Robin, based on stories created by the family about his favourite stuffed toys. Milne was disappointed when his publisher first suggested Shepard as an illustrator (he thought he was 'perfectly hopeless'), but thankfully changed his mind after Shepard had sketched Christopher Robin and some of his toys: Kanga, Roo, Tigger, Eeyore and Piglet. Thus began a collaboration between artist and writer that would result in these enduring images, which are of course perfectly perfect for the text.

SHRINKING TERRITORY

In the last hundred years, we have lost 90 per cent of the world's tigers and three of the subspecies. Between 1930 and 1980 the last of the Balinese, Caspian and Javan tigers were shot and they have all been declared extinct. There are now more tigers in captivity than in the wild and many of these are in private ownership in the United States. Some could argue that this is the best place for them, given that we cannot be trusted to protect them in the wild. However, in the wild, tigers have space, challenge and a choice of partners. Rearing cubs that will become independent takes place naturally. In captivity, breeding raises all sorts of problems. What do you do with the cubs once they need to be separated from their mother? How do you ensure a varied gene pool while keeping the genetic purity of the subspecies? Some zoos manage this very successfully and have raised large sums of money for conservation, but the the future is not looking orange ... the future is looking pretty grim.

Tigers can only survive in the wild if people value them as living independent creatures, allowed some privacy and allowed to keep their bones and whiskers until they have finished with them.

Tiger's range in 1900

Tiger's range today

Approximate numbers in the wild

Indian (Bengal)	3–5,000
Indochinese	1–2,000
Sumatran	400–600
Amur (Siberian)	400
South China	possibly extinct

THANK YOU

Thank you for buying this book

Thanks to the generosity of the Simon Gibson Charitable Trust, The Iliffe Family Charitable Trust, the Manifold Trust and the Rothschild Foundation (who have supported the production costs), income from these books will go to 21st Century Tiger to help save tigers in the wild. If you have bought the book directly from 21st Century Tiger, then 50 per cent of the cover price will go to them. If you have bought it from a bookshop, then any profit will go to 21st Century Tiger. Unfortunately, millions of pounds are required to protect tigers in their different habitats, so please buy a few more ...

21st Century Tiger

This is a conservation partnership between the Zoological Society of London and Global Tiger Patrol. It spends 100 per cent of donations it receives on conservation projects that support tigers in the wild – in the Russian Far East, Indonesia, India and China. Each project must have scientific and conservation value and use local staff wherever possible. Projects are selected by an international panel of tiger experts and reviewed regularly to meet ever-changing environmental situations. *For further information, you can visit their website: www.21stCenturyTiger.org*

Rhino

If you have enjoyed this book, please look out for one on the rhino, also published by Silver Jungle. Profits from that book go to Save the Rhino International to help protect a small species with furry ears living in Sumatra. The book can be ordered from *www.savetherhino.org* or from your local bookshop.

And thank you

Many friends have helped with advice and encouragement but there are some who have played a very large role in the production of this book.

Particular thanks to Quentin Newark for his long-standing support and George Gibson for his continued interest in the project.

Thank you to Hermès in London for their contribution towards picture costs.

Many thanks also to Nicholas Serota, Martin Holman, Annabel Ossel, Ian McHale, Dido Sheffield, Sarah Christie, Jane Morris, Slaney Begley, Paola Faoro, Tom Hope, Stephen Coates, Elisabeth Scheder-Bieschin, Matilda Moreton, Nat Jansz, Elizabeth Skipwith, Annabel Huxley, Cathy Dean, Libby Wiener, Natasha Seery and John Nicoll.

Finally in the great roll-call tradition, many thanks to Patrick and Gabriel and to my husband, Simon, who supports the wildlife living under his roof as well as the tiger and the rhino.

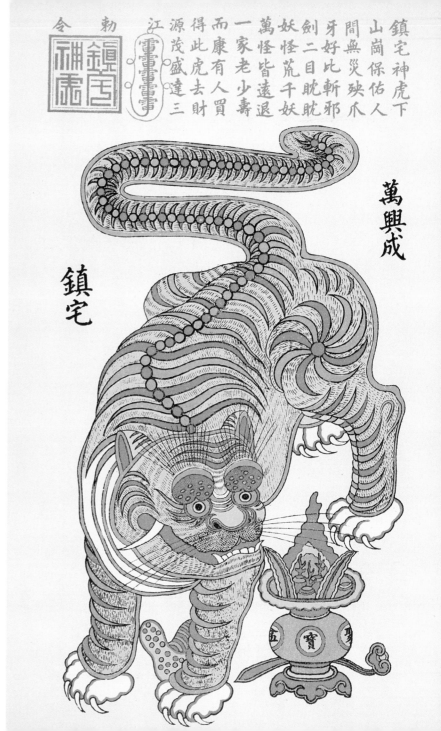

The briefest of bibliographies
I have consulted many books and am
very grateful to the public service offered
by ZSL, the British Library, the Linnean
Society and the Natural History Library.
Many thanks to those who have written
such interesting books about tigers,
among them Valmik Thapar, Guy
Mountfort and Richard Perry.

Thanks also to some excellent websites,
in particular:
www.savethetigerfund.org
and *www.lairweb.org.nz*
(warning: it will roar at you)

Chinese artist
Tiger amulet, guardian of the treasure
Illustration for Henri Doré's
Superstitions en Chine, volume 2, 1912
(The artist's name is not given)

Published by Silver Jungle Ltd
PO Box 51793, London NW1W 9AZ

©Joanna Skipwith and
Silver Jungle Ltd 2006

ISBN
0-9552652-0-7
978-0-9552652-0-4

Picture Credits

If not credited below, images have been
supplied by the owner or artist listed in
the caption. Every effort has been made
to clear all copyrights. If anyone has been
overlooked, please write to Silver Jungle
Ltd, PO Box 51793, London NW1W 9AZ.

The Art Archive
p. 7 The Art Archive/Museo Nazionale
delle Terme, Rome/Dagli Orti

Bridgeman Art Library
p. 17 Landseer, 19 Rousseau, 29 Rubens,
33 Fatal Combat, 37 Dalí ©Salvador Dalí,
Gala-Salvador Dalí Foundation, DACS,
London 2006

Christie's Images Ltd
p. 11 Wilson, 31 Khwan Plykeaw-Barton

Jonathan Cooper Gallery
p. 15 Stinton

Mary Evans Picture Library
p. 5 detail from *The Hare and the Tiger*
in *Folk-tales from Tibet*
p. 47 *Tiger amulet*

Map
p. 45 drawn by Roger Taylor
©Silver Jungle Ltd

Réunion des musées nationaux, Paris
p. 23 ©Photo RMN/©Michèle Bellot

Riotip, Khabarovsk, Russia
p. 25 courtesy of Oleg Starikov

V&A Images
p. 35, p. 43 colour sketch for *The World
of Pooh*, published by E.P. Hutton,
New York, 1957, and by Methuen & Co.
Ltd, London, 1958. Colour plate ©1958
E.H. Shepard, reproduced by permission
of Curtis Brown Group Ltd, London

The tiger that creeps into the book on
page 2 and creeps out here was drawn
by Pulak Biswas, an Indian artist.
More of the tiger appears in his book
Tiger on a Tree, published by Tara Books
in 1997.